OPLE AT
CENTER OF

THE AMERICAN REVOLUTION

By GAIL B. STEWART

BLACKBIRCH™
PRESS

THOMSON

San Diego • Detroit • New York • San Francisco • Cleveland
New Haven, Conn. • Waterville, Maine • London • Munich

LIBRARY OF CONGRESS CATALOGING-IN-PUBLICATION DATA

Stewart, Gail, 1949-
  The American Revolution / by Gail B. Stewart.
    p. cm. — (People at the center of:)
Summary: Profiles people involved in the Revolutionary War as soldiers, politicians, or in
other capacities, including King George II, Benedict Arnold, and Mary Hays McCauly
(Molly Pitcher).
Includes bibliographical references and index.
  ISBN 1-56711-769-4 (hardcover : alk. paper)
  1. United States—History—Revolution, 1775-1783—Juvenile literature. [1. United
States—History—Revolution, 1775-1783—Biography.] I. Title. II. Series.

E208.S86 2004
973.3'092'2—dc22   2003013656

Contents

PEOPLE AT THE CENTER OF

THE AMERICAN REVOLUTION

The American Revolution, also called the War of Independence, was an event that marked the end of thirteen English colonies and the beginning of the United States of America. It was not a war over disputed boundaries, as so many wars are. It was not fought because of religious or cultural differences. It was fought because the American colonies no longer wanted to be controlled by Britain, and Britain was not willing to give up that control.

The tension and rebellion that erupted into war in April 1775 had been building for years. In the mid-1760s, King George III and his ministers enacted a series of laws meant to increase money coming into Britain. The British had just finished a seven-year war with the French in America. Even though the British had won the war, the large amounts of money needed to sustain the army for that long had drained the British treasury. Lack of money resulted in record-high unemployment and a foundering economy—the modern equivalent of $30 billion of national debt.

The colonists were resentful of the new laws that placed taxes on items that had never before been taxed. Many colonial leaders felt that since they had no representative in Parliament, where the laws were made, that such taxes were morally wrong. "No taxation without representation" became a slogan used frequently by colonists.

One such law, the Stamp Act of 1765, was extremely unpopular. The act had put a tax on any paper used in the colonies—any legal form, any newspaper, and even decks of playing cards. When the colonists refused to pay the tax and threatened to boycott British goods, the British realized it would be impossible to enforce and repealed it a year after it was passed.

Many colonists responded angrily to the Stamp Act of 1765, which taxed every piece of paper they used. Tensions over new British taxes grew until the outbreak of the American Revolution.

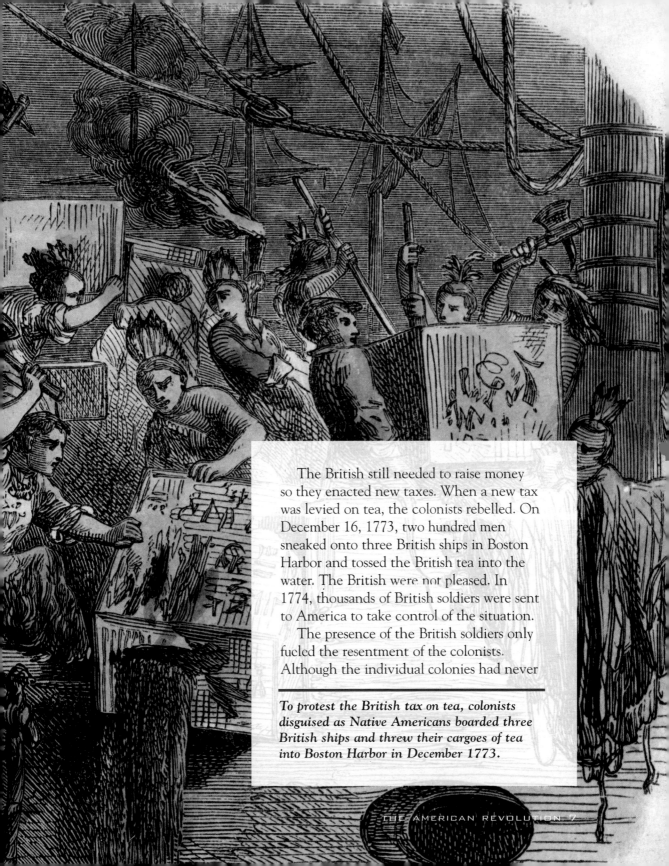

The British still needed to raise money so they enacted new taxes. When a new tax was levied on tea, the colonists rebelled. On December 16, 1773, two hundred men sneaked onto three British ships in Boston Harbor and tossed the British tea into the water. The British were not pleased. In 1774, thousands of British soldiers were sent to America to take control of the situation.

The presence of the British soldiers only fueled the resentment of the colonists. Although the individual colonies had never

To protest the British tax on tea, colonists disguised as Native Americans boarded three British ships and threw their cargoes of tea into Boston Harbor in December 1773.

This illustration depicts the Battle of Lexington, where the first shots of the American Revolution were fired in April 1775.

gotten along well before, they decided to form a Continental Congress to find ways to defend their rights. At the same time, colonists began to stockpile weapons and ammunition in case a war with the British troops broke out.

It was the stockpiling of weapons that resulted in the first battles of the war. A British commander who heard that a large stash of weapons was located in two villages north of Boston—Lexington and Concord—gave the order for his troops to confiscate the weapons. Colonial spies heard of the plan, however, and alerted militias throughout the area. When the British marched on Lexington and Concord late on the night of April 18, 1775, they were met by armed American patriots. The British yelled for the men to lay down their weapons, but the militias refused. Shots were fired, and the war began.

It was a war, say historians, that few believed could be won by the colonies. For one thing, Britain in the 1700s had undisputed power. Its army was mighty, and the British navy was without equal. The American colonies, however, had almost nothing. They had no army and no navy. The only fighting forces were a collection

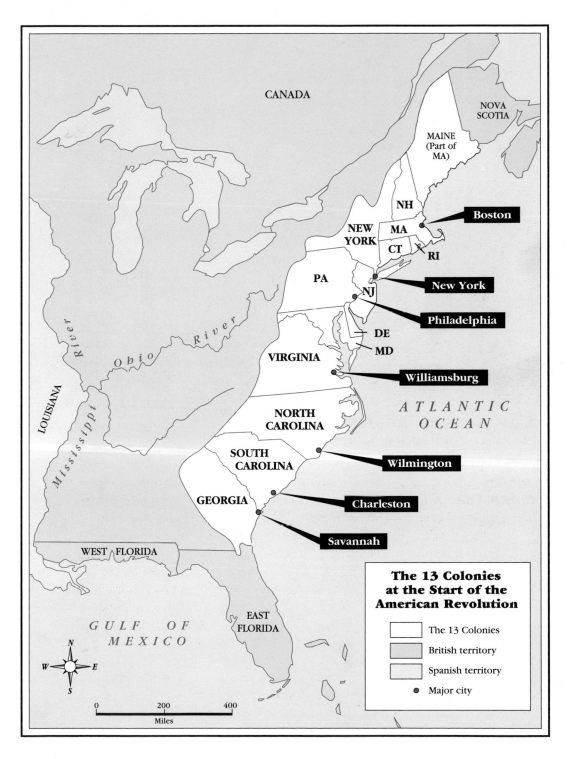

CANADA

NOVA SCOTIA

MAINE (Part of MA)

NH

NEW YORK

MA

CT

RI

Boston

PA

NJ

New York

Philadelphia

DE

MD

VIRGINIA

Williamsburg

NORTH CAROLINA

ATLANTIC OCEAN

SOUTH CAROLINA

Wilmington

GEORGIA

Charleston

Savannah

LOUISIANA

Mississippi River

Ohio River

WEST FLORIDA

EAST FLORIDA

GULF OF MEXICO

N W E S

0   200   400
Miles

The 13 Colonies at the Start of the American Revolution

☐ The 13 Colonies

☐ British territory

☐ Spanish territory

● Major city

Opposite: A painting depicts Benjamin Franklin, John Adams, and Thomas Jefferson (left to right) as they draft the Declaration of Independence. Above: The Continental army was so poorly equipped that many soldiers, who lacked proper clothing, died from exposure to the cold.

of state and local volunteer militias, much like the ones who confronted the British at Lexington and Concord.

Although the Continental Congress had been formed to unite the colonies, it did not have the authority to tax each colony to raise money. As a result, when the new Continental army was formed in 1775, it was difficult to provide the soldiers even with basics, such as ammunition, food rations, and uniforms.

The lack of funds to support the army made the war that much more one-sided. In several battles, Continental soldiers could fire their muskets only three or four times because of a shortage of gunpowder. During the winter of 1778, one-fourth of the Continental army died because of malnutrition, exposure to the cold brought on by lack of warm clothing, and disease. It was the most poorly equipped army in history.

In spite of what appeared at first to be a one-sided conflict, the Revolutionary War stretched on for six long years. It was fought in cities like New York and Boston, in southern mountain areas, and at sea. It involved the two armies as well as Native Americans and settlers in the most remote parts of the American frontier.

The result was a victory for the Americans, who were no longer colonists, but citizens of a new nation. They had fought for their independence from Britain and achieved it.

George III of England was born in London on June 4, 1738, when his grandfather, George II, was king. He became heir to the throne at age thirteen, when his father, Frederick, prince of Wales, died. He became King George III when his grandfather died nine years later. The young king had not been a good student, and his inability to come up with thoughtful solutions to problems created difficulties during his reign.

A pressing issue for George was the lack of money in England's treasury. His ministers suggested levying taxes on the colonists in America as a way to bring in money, and George supported the plan. On the other hand, the colonists believed that because they were not represented in Parliament—and therefore could not vote on such taxes—they should not have to pay. George was furious, for he thought the colonies were becoming insubordinate and unruly. When his ministers suggested levying yet another tax—this one on tea, a favorite beverage in the colonies— he supported that tax, too.

When, in 1773, a group of men sneaked onto three British ships in Boston Harbor and threw their cargoes of tea into the harbor, George had had enough. He sent British troops to America and warned them to keep control of the colonies. Many historians say that if both sides had sat down together and discussed the issues, the war might have been avoided. When the newly formed Continental Congress sent the king a petition that requested more independence in their own affairs, however, George was unwilling even to read it.

By April 1775, fighting had broken out between the British army and bands of colonists, and relations between America and England deteriorated even further. Because the colonists believed that it was important to explain to King George why they were seeking freedom from England, they sent him the Declaration of Independence in July 1776. King George considered the colonists rebels, however, and he refused to consider their demands.

The stresses of the war put a great strain on King George's health, and he had bouts of a disease, known today as porphyria, that causes physical pain and severe mental instability. By 1811, he had become mentally unfit. His son George IV took over the throne, and nine years later, in 1820, George III died.

King George III imposed unpopular taxes on the colonies and refused to consider their demands for independence.

Benjamin Franklin was born on January 17, 1706, in Boston. The fifteenth in a family of seventeen children, he began work at age ten as a candle maker in his father's shop. He ran away to Philadelphia when he was seventeen and became a printer. Although he had not attended school very long, he had a quick mind, and in his spare time taught himself science, math, and philosophy. A witty and interesting writer, Franklin started a newspaper, the *Philadelphia Gazette*.

Franklin's involvement with the Revolutionary War started long before the fighting began. He believed that if the thirteen colonies united they would be much stronger against their enemies, and he wrote on the subject in his newspaper. He was elected to the Pennsylvania legislature in 1736 and was chosen postmaster for all of the colonies in 1753. In 1757, the legislature sent him to London to settle a tax dispute, and he remained in London for fifteen years. He was so diplomatic that his opinions about the disputes between the colonies and the British government were listened to with respect.

As relations between the colonies and England worsened, however, even Franklin's diplomatic opinions were no longer listened to by the British. He returned home about the time the war began in the spring of 1775. He became involved in the Continental Congress and formulated plans to collect money from individual colonies and to find munitions and other supplies. He also served on the committee with John Adams, an important lawyer from Massachusetts, and Thomas Jefferson, the youngest member of the Continental Congress, to draft the Declaration of Independence. One of Franklin's most important contributions of that time was his service as the colonies' ambassador to France. He persuaded the French to sign a treaty of alliance with the colonies and to supply soldiers and money to the American cause.

He returned to America in 1785 after he helped write the Treaty of Paris, which officially ended the war. By this time he was eighty years old—a very old man by eighteenth-century standards. Even so, he was anxious to be a part of the convention that drafted the first U.S. Constitution. Historians say that because of his presence at the convention, the colonies' disputes with one another were settled more peacefully. He died on April 17, 1790.

Benjamin Franklin helped to draft the Declaration of Independence and secured France's support for the American war effort. Franklin's wit and diplomacy made him one of America's most beloved statesmen.

Thomas Paine was born on January 29, 1737, in Norfolk County, England. As a young man, he was not interested in becoming a corset maker like his father. He enjoyed thinking about politics and philosophy and began to write essays and pamphlets about topics such as taxes and poverty.

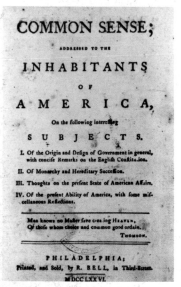

Thomas Paine (opposite) wrote Common Sense *(above), a booklet that argued for the colonies' independence. His lucid, direct writing style inspired even George Washington.*

While in London, Paine met Benjamin Franklin, the American diplomat who was trying to keep peace between England and the colonies. Franklin urged Paine to go to America, for there were people there who were thinking about the same issues he wrote about. In 1774, Paine arrived in Philadelphia. He got a job as a contributing editor to the *Pennsylvania Magazine* and wrote essays that supported the idea of independence from England.

In January 1776, Paine wrote a forty-two-page booklet called *Common Sense*. To him, it seemed obvious that the colonies should be free and that people should have equal rights under the law. In his booklet, he criticizes King George and his ministers and applauds those voices in America that call for freedom. The booklet became an instant success—and the first American best seller. More than 120,000 copies were printed and sold in twelve weeks. There is no doubt that *Common Sense*, written in simple but powerful language, did much to rouse people to believe in the cause of independence.

In December 1776, he wrote another booklet, *The American Crisis*, in which he explains that the process of such a revolution is difficult and long. This was a hard time for America, for there had been few victories in recent months, and many were starting to doubt whether victory was possible. Again, his words were so inspiring that George Washington urged his soldiers to read the booklet.

After the war, Paine went to France, for his pamphlets were popular with those French who hoped to have their own revolution. In the violence that followed the French Revolution, however, Paine was jailed. Only intervention by the U.S. ambassador in France freed him. He returned to the United States in 1802 and died in 1804.

Thomas Jefferson was born on April 13, 1743, on a large Virginia plantation called Shadwell. He became a lawyer and built his own estate, called Monticello, after he inherited land from his father at the age of twenty-six. In addition to practicing law, Jefferson became interested in politics and served in Virginia's legislature, the House of Burgesses.

A strong believer that the American colonies should be independent, Jefferson was elected in 1775 to the newly formed Continental Congress. Although Jefferson was one of the youngest delegates to the Continental Congress, he was one of the most respected because of his quick mind and easy way with words. When the Congress decided to declare the colonies' independence from England in 1776, Jefferson was chosen to write the declaration, with the help of John Adams, a brilliant lawyer from Massachusetts, and Benjamin Franklin, who had served as a diplomat in England before the war began.

Thomas Jefferson (left), one of Continental Congress's youngest delegates, authored the Declaration of Independence (above). He became president of the United States in 1800.

Jefferson worked alone for days to create the first draft of the document. In it, Jefferson wrote that all men are created equal and that government can only derive power from the consent of those being governed. The Declaration of Independence, as it was called, was so well written that it became one of the most famous documents ever written—as well as an inspiration to other nations who desired liberty. On July 4, 1776, the Declaration of Independence was read and approved by the delegates to the Continental Congress. The original was signed by the delegates and sent to King George III, while thousands of copies were printed and distributed throughout the colonies.

After the war ended in 1782, Jefferson succeeded Franklin as the ambassador to France, and when his friend George Washington was chosen to be president in 1789, Jefferson became the nation's first secretary of state. He defeated Adams in the 1800 presidential election, and served for eight years. He retired to Monticello and died on July 4, 1826. Coincidentally, he died on the fiftieth anniversary of the signing of the Declaration of Independence, and his friend and cosigner, John Adams, died a few hours later.

GEORGE WASHINGTON

LED THE CONTINENTAL ARMY TO VICTORY

George Washington was born on February 22, 1732, in Westmoreland County, Virginia. The son of a wealthy tobacco farmer. Washington trained to be a surveyor until he joined the British army at age twenty-two. He fought against the French and their Indian allies in what became known later as the French and Indian Wars—essentially, a dispute over territory in America. After he distinguished himself as a fine soldier, Washington married and looked forward to a peaceful life of farming in Virginia.

When the American colonies rose up in rebellion against the British, however, Washington was called into service once more. On June 15, 1775, he was chosen by the colonial leaders to command the Continental army and fight against the British. He agreed, but insisted that he would take no money for the job, as he knew the Congress had little money to spend.

When Washington took command on July 3, 1775, he quickly realized how difficult his new job would be. The ragtag collection of volunteers who had fought British troops at Lexington and Concord were mostly farmers, most of whom had no military training or even experience firing a gun. In many battles, these soldiers turned and ran when they saw approaching British soldiers.

General George Washington (opposite) led the Continental army to victory despite the inexperience of his troops and a lack of food, clothing, and ammunition. After the war, Washington returned to Mount Vernon (above), his Virginia estate.

The lack of experienced soldiers was only one of Washington's problems. Because of the inability of the Continental Congress to collect money from the colonies, they could not provide Washington and his men with enough food, ammunition, and clothing. In fact, several battles were lost because his men had no gunpowder. Even with such hardships, Washington used kindness, discipline, and leadership to make his troops into a real army, to which the British surrendered on October 19, 1781, at Yorktown, Virginia, and ended the war.

After the war, Washington was happy to return to Mount Vernon, his estate in Virginia. He was called back into service, however—not as a military man, but as the first president of the United States. He served eight years. Washington died on December 14, 1799.

This illustration depicts Washington as he takes the oath of office and becomes the first president of the United States of America.

John Adams was born in Braintree, Massachusetts, on October 19, 1735. Although he was not fond of school as a child, he knew he did not want to be a farmer. He graduated from college after working as a schoolteacher for a time, and he eventually became a lawyer.

Adams was furious when, in 1765, the British Stamp Act was passed. It levied a tax on any printed paper purchased by the colonists. Adams was a strong voice in his Massachusetts community against the tax, and because he was a good lawyer, people listened and many refused to pay the tax.

When the colonies decided to send delegates to the first Continental Congress in 1774, Adams was chosen for Massachusetts. He was an influential member of the Congress, and although sometimes aloof or brusque with people, he was dedicated to the idea of independence. Adams persuaded the other delegates to authorize the creation of a Continental army, and then suggested George Washington, the well-known soldier from Virginia, as the army's commander.

John Adams (opposite) strongly supported the war effort and helped draft the Declaration of Independence. He was the first president to live in the White House (above).

In 1776, Adams was part of a committee to work on the Declaration of Independence. Although it was Thomas Jefferson who wrote it, Adams was the man chosen to read it to the Congress on July 2, 1776. He spoke tirelessly in his efforts to convince the delegates that the Declaration should be ratified. In large part because of his efforts, it was ratified on July 4, 1776.

As the war continued, Adams helped the army enormously. He served on a committee called the Board of War and Ordnance, which organized the shipments of food, uniforms, and ammunition to the soldiers. It was a difficult job, for the Congress had no real authority to collect money from the individual colonies.

After the war, Adams was sent as a representative in the peace negotiations with England and France, and in 1783 was made American ambassador to Holland. Three years later, he was sent to Britain to try to establish trade with the British. In 1788, he returned to the United States. He served as vice president under president George Washington, and in 1797, became president—the first to live in the White House, which was completed in 1800. He died in 1826.

THOMAS GAGE

LED BRITISH TROOPS IN THE FIRST BATTLE OF THE WAR

Thomas Gage was born in Firle, England, in 1721. His father was a nobleman and helped his son get a good start on becoming a military officer. In those days, it was almost impossible to advance to the higher ranks of the military without connections. Gage accompanied a group of British forces to America in 1754. The French were trying to take over important territory previously staked out by the British, and the British forces were sent to reclaim it.

Gage served with distinction, and in 1760 he was made governor of Montreal in Canada, a British possession. Three years later he was promoted again—this time to the rank of commander in chief of North America. In 1774, there was growing unrest in the American colonies. When some colonists sneaked aboard three British ships in Boston Harbor and emptied their cargoes of tea into the water to protest a new tax on tea, King George imposed several new laws on the Massachusetts colony, which included the closing of Boston Harbor until the colonists paid for the tea that was destroyed.

Colonists called this law, and others that accompanied it, the Intolerable Acts. Aware that the acts would be protested by the colony, King George sent Gage and four thousand soldiers to make certain the laws were obeyed. Even though Gage was personally a pleasant man, the colonists in Boston, resentful of his presence and that of the British soldiers, gave him a cold welcome.

By the spring of 1775, Gage had information that some colonists were stealing ammunition and weapons from British arsenals. The largest stash of weapons was in the area of Lexington and Concord, two villages northwest of Boston. When Gage and his troops began a secret march toward the villages to seize the weapons before dawn on April 19, 1775, a group of militia groups confronted them. Shots were fired, and the war was on.

Gage survived the fighting at Lexington and Concord, and later commanded troops in the Battle of Bunker Hill. While the British eventually forced the Americans to retreat, more than one thousand British soldiers under Gage's command were killed. The was so costly, Gage was recalled to England by the British government. He died in 1787.

King George sent Thomas Gage (opposite) to the colonies to ensure compliance with British laws. Gage and his troops later fought colonists in the first battles of the Revolutionary War.

Abigail Smith was born in Massachusetts on November 11, 1744. She had no formal education, for at that time few girls had the opportunity to attend school. Smith was frequently ill as a child and took advantage of the time to read books from her father's extensive library on almost every subject, which included philosophy, poetry, drama, and politics.

In 1764, she married John Adams, a lawyer, and established their home on a farm in Braintree, Massachusetts. Now Abigail Adams, she had five children in eight years, and while her husband traveled throughout New England and pursued his career as a lawyer, she remained in Braintree. In 1768, they moved to Boston, where there was a great deal of talk about the colonies' independence from England. She was delighted when, in 1774, her husband was elected as a delegate to the colonies' newly formed legislative body, the Continental Congress. Even though it meant that she and John would be apart more often, she believed it was important that he work for independence.

When her husband John was away on business, Abigail Adams (opposite) ran their home in Massachusetts (above) and wrote him letters of encouragement and advice.

Like many colonial women during the war, she had to assume many more responsibilities. John was frequently in Philadelphia, where the Congress met. When she and her children returned to Braintree for the duration of the war, Adams alone took care of the farm, the children, and the family finances. In addition, she kept up a constant written correspondence with John. They shared their ideas about the war, about their children and friends, and how much they missed one another. When John was drafting laws concerning rights and freedoms of the Americans, Adams wrote emphatically that he and his fellow delegates should remember to assign those rights to women, too.

John was elected president in 1797, and in 1800 Adams became the first First Lady to live in the new White House. After she suffered from ill health for a number of years, she died on October 28, 1818—seven years before her son, John Quincy Adams, became the nation's sixth president.

Benedict Arnold was born on January 14, 1741, in Norwich, Connecticut. He opened an apothecary shop (similar to a drugstore) in New Haven, Connecticut, when he was a young man. He was a good businessman, and within five years he was one of the wealthiest men in town. Like many men, Arnold served in his state militia, which was an all-volunteer group. When war broke out, he gladly enlisted in the Continental army and became a colonel.

Arnold's army career began gloriously. On May 10, 1775, together with New Hampshire soldier Ethan Allen, Arnold led the capture of Fort Ticonderoga, an important British fort on Lake Champlain in upstate New York. He also led an expedition of more than one thousand soldiers into British Canada to attack Quebec, the capital city. Although the assault was not successful, Arnold's courage in battle won the respect of many, including George Washington, commander of the Continental army. He was promoted to brigadier general, and for the next five years took part in a number of important battles. In the battle of Saratoga in September 1777, Arnold led a daring attack on the middle of the British line. Although he was seriously wounded in the leg, he contributed greatly to an important victory for the Continental army.

This nineteenth-century lithograph depicts the discovery of the letter that detailed Benedict Arnold's plan to surrender West Point to the British.

Arnold had problems that interfered with his successes, however. He was often angry because he felt others were getting more attention and better promotions. In addition, when he turned in his list of expenses to the Congress, the amounts were often suspiciously high. Disgusted with the Continental Congress and bitter about not being appreciated by his peers, Arnold did something that all but erased the good name he had earned as a military leader: He committed treason.

In 1780, Arnold asked to take control of West Point, which was then a fort and barracks for many soldiers in the Continental army. He wrote a letter to British

commander Sir Henry Clinton and promised that he would surrender West Point in return for twenty thousand pounds sterling (the equivalent of $1 million today). Later, the British messenger carrying papers from Arnold to Clinton was captured, and Arnold's crime was uncovered. Arnold escaped to New York, where he fought as a British officer.

Arnold began a merchant business in England after the war. He died in London in 1801.

Benedict Arnold enjoyed a distinguished career as a colonel in the Continental army. When he felt unappreciated, however, Arnold betrayed his country.

FRANCIS MARION

EARNED THE NICKNAME THE SWAMP FOX

Francis Marion was born around 1732 on a plantation in what is now Georgetown, South Carolina. The plantation was surrounded by swamps, and as a boy he enjoyed going out on his own to explore them. As a young man, he was a farmer until fighting broke out between settlers and the native Cherokee in 1759. He became a part of the cavalry, and afterward was elected to the South Carolina legislature.

Marion's ancestors, French protestants, had come to South Carolina in 1690 seeking religious freedom, so it was not surprising that Marion supported the idea of independence from England. In 1775, he was part of the local legislature that condemned England's taxes on the colony. When fighting broke out, he served in his state militia and in 1776 drove British troops out of Charleston, the most important seaport in South Carolina. The British recaptured the city in May 1780, however. Marion and a few soldiers escaped to the swamps, but most of his men were killed or taken prisoner.

By August 1780, it seemed that British troops were in control of the area. With a small army of only about sixty men, Marion could not fight in open battle. Instead, he and his men used guerrilla tactics—they ambushed British patrols, freed American prisoners, and sniped at British patrols from hiding places. If British forces

Francis Marion (opposite) used guerrilla tactics to frustrate British efforts to control South Carolina. His skillful navigation of swamps (above) earned Marion the nickname the Swamp Fox.

chased them, they merely ran to the swamps and found places to disappear. It was a British general who gave Marion his nickname, the "Swamp Fox." As the war continued, Marion and his soldiers attracted more local followers. They made raids on British supply depots and interfered so much that historians give them credit for keeping the British troops from sweeping through the South and into Virginia. Had that happened, the war might well have gone on longer, and with different results.

After the war ended in October 1781, Marion returned to his farm. He agreed to serve several terms in the South Carolina senate and was part of the legislative process that made South Carolina the eighth state of the Union. He died in 1795.

Lafayette was born in Haute-Loire, France, on September 6, 1757. His father had been a soldier and died when Lafayette was only two years old. The stories of his father's bravery made the boy eager to be a soldier himself. He went to school at the Military Academy at Versailles and became a captain in the French cavalry.

This was a fairly peaceful time in French history, however, and Lafayette did not have opportunities to prove himself in battle. He wanted to join General George Washington's Continental army, because the idea of fighting for freedom alongside the rebellious colonists appealed to him. He met with the American ambassador to France, Benjamin Franklin, in 1776, and Franklin quickly wrote to Washington about the promising nineteen-year-old.

Although his family was angry that he was going abroad, Lafayette and ten other soldiers who sought adventure sailed for America in April 1777. Lafayette had hoped to join the army as a paid officer, but it was clear when he arrived that the Continental army could not afford to pay him. Lafayette, who had inherited a great deal of money when his father died, did not care about the money. He offered to fight as a volunteer and joined Washington's staff.

Lafayette proved himself a talented soldier and leader, even though he was far younger than many of the men he commanded. He soon was given command of a division. He fought in several key battles, including the Battle of Monmouth, an important battle in New Jersey in 1778 that showed how strong the Continental army had become.

He returned to France in the spring of 1779 and helped persuade the French government to send more aid to the Americans. In 1780, he continued his service in the Continental army back in America. Lafayette's division helped cut off the escape route of British general Charles Cornwallis in Virginia in 1781, which allowed Washington's forces to defeat the British at Yorktown. Following that battle, Cornwallis surrendered on October 19, 1781, which ended the war.

Lafayette left America as a hero and returned to France in 1782. He was made commander of the French National Guard, and although he was a supporter of liberty and freedom, extremists imprisoned Lafayette during the French Revolution. He was freed in 1797, and when Napoléon Bonaparte was crowned emperor of France in 1804, Lafayette served in France's legislative body, the Chamber of Deputies. He died in 1834.

In April 1777, the Marquis de Lafayette left France to join the Continental army. He became an effective commander and led his troops to several important victories.

MARY HAYS MCCAULEY

It is not known for certain what Mary Hays McCauley's maiden name was or where or when she was born, but it is believed by historians that she was born about 1754 near Philadelphia. She worked as a servant in Carlisle, Pennsylvania, when she was just a teen and married the village barber, William Hays.

William enlisted as an artilleryman in the Philadelphia regiment of the Continental army when war broke out in 1775. His job was to load and fire some of the largest cannons. Like many women from the lower and middle classes, Mary Hays could not support herself; so she chose to accompany her husband and follow the army as one of a group of wives who helped cook and sew for the soldiers. During battles, Hays would also bring pitchers of water to the crews of artillerymen— not only to drink, but to cool the cannon barrels between firings.

Mary Hays McCauley (opposite) gained fame after she took her incapacitated husband's place at a cannon during the Battle of Monmouth (above).

Hays's fame came from the Battle of Monmouth, on June 28, 1778. It was a particularly hot day, and the additional heat produced by the cannons resulted in heatstroke for her husband and others. Without William in position, the cannon was useless, and that put the rest of the crew in danger. Hays felt that she knew how the crews worked, so she took William's place behind the cannon. The battle ended in a stalemate, but George Washington was pleased that his men had done well against the strong British forces.

Hays, or Molly Pitcher, as the men fondly called her, was praised by Washington for her courage. At the end of the war, she and William returned to Pennsylvania. After William died in 1789, she married George McCauley, a soldier who had been a friend of William. In 1823, she was honored by the Pennsylvania legislature with a pension of forty dollars yearly for service to her country. She died in 1832 in Carlisle.

Nathan Hale was born in Coventry, Connecticut, on June 6, 1755. The sixth of twelve children in the family, he attended Yale College and went on to teach school after graduation. Hale was a fervent believer in the cause of liberty, and when the war began in April 1775, he met with his students, shook their hands, and left to fight the British.

He was made first lieutenant in the Connecticut regiment and helped drive the British from Boston in March 1776. Later, the regiment moved to New York, where Hale and his men set fire to a British boat, *Phoenix*, and destroyed cannons and other weapons on board. Hale's role in that attack brought him to the attention of military leaders, who established the Rangers, a special force that included Hale and other extremely talented soldiers. The Rangers took their orders directly from George Washington, and did sabotage, spying, and reconnaissance, or observation of British troops, for the Continental army. Soon the Rangers became respected by soldiers as the elite fighting force of the army.

In September 1776, Washington was frustrated at not knowing exactly where the British army would move next. Because he did not have enough men or ammunition to split his army to cover two possible British routes, Washington asked the Rangers' commander to choose a soldier who could pass through the enemy lines and get information about the British army's plans. The mission was risky, for any spy who was caught was automatically hanged. Even so, Hale volunteered. He left his uniform at camp and traveled as a civilian Connecticut schoolmaster.

He got the information, but on the way back, he was seized. Hale had made notes on the British army's strength and plans and had hidden them in his shoes, and they were discovered. He was sent by boat back to New York, where he spent the night of September 21 in jail. He asked his guards for paper and pen, so that he could write to his mother and a fellow officer. The executioner destroyed the letters, however, and on the morning of September 22, Hale was hanged. Just before the execution, he was told to apologize for his crime. No one knows Hale's response, although he is credited by some legends as saying bravely, "I only regret that I have but one life to lose for my country."

Convicted of spying, an unapologetic Nathan Hale (opposite, in white) was hanged by the British on September 22, 1776.

Friedrich Wilhelm von Steuben was born in 1730 in Prussia, which was a kingdom in Europe made up of what is now northern Germany and Poland. Von Steuben's father was in the army, and by age seventeen, von Steuben was himself an officer in the Prussian military. His abilities were outstanding, and he was eventually given an assignment in the headquarters of the ruler of Prussia, Frederick the Great.

When von Steuben was discharged from the army, he visited Paris in 1777. There he met Benjamin Franklin, the American ambassador to France. Von Steuben was interested in going to America to help the colonists, and Franklin wrote a grand letter of recommendation to General George Washington. Von Steuben arrived in the colonies in the fall of 1777, and after he spoke to members of the Continental Congress, he agreed to volunteer his services training the soldiers until money was available.

Baron von Steuben (opposite) was an outstanding Prussian military officer. Von Steuben (above, second from left) helped Washington (above, left) train Continental soldiers.

In February 1778, he joined Washington's forces at their winter quarters in Valley Forge, just twenty-two miles from Philadelphia. Von Steuben had learned a great deal working for Frederick the Great, who was considered a military genius. Though Washington's soldiers had had some success, their strength was in shooting from behind rocks and trees rather than fighting in formation. Not every battle could be fought like that, so von Steuben taught them to work and fight as a unit, to respond to precision commands, to load their weapons quickly, and especially to use the bayonet—a knife at the end of the musket—which most were unfamiliar with. Von Steuben spoke no English, but he could speak French, which a few of the officers understood.

Despite the language barrier, the new skills transformed the Continental army. Their ability to fight as a unit helped them at the Battle of Monmouth in June 1778. Washington recommended that von Steuben be given the title of inspector general, and Congress approved it. The following winter, von Steuben wrote a manual, known as the *Blue Book*, of techniques that the American forces should all master.

After the war, von Steuben assisted Washington in the demobilization of the army—releasing them gradually to civilian life. He became an American citizen in 1784 and set up a home in New York. He died in 1794.

JOHN PAUL JONES

John Paul was born in Scotland on July 6, 1747. He was eager to be a sailor, and at thirteen was apprenticed on the ship *Friendship*. On a 1773 voyage, his crew committed mutiny and, in self-defense, Jones killed the ringleader of the rebellion. Paul's friends urged him to run away to Virginia, which he did. John Paul added the "Jones" to his name to hide his true identity.

While still in Europe, Jones had met Benjamin Franklin, who was trying to recruit talented European sea captains for service in America. British ships were firing cannonballs on American coastal towns, and the colonies were without a navy to drive them off. Franklin urged Jones to go to Philadelphia to meet with another leader, John Adams, who served on the committee that was trying to build a navy. Jones was eager to fight and was given the rank of lieutenant in the new Continental navy in 1775.

Jones knew that the American navy could not defeat the British navy, but they could do some damage. He and his crews waged war on

As a lieutenant in the Continental navy, John Paul Jones (opposite) led the crew of the Bonhomme Richard *in many attacks on British ships (above).*

the British navy—not in the waters off American shores, but near England. They lobbed cannonballs at many British ships in port, and when the British gave chase, Jones and his crew sailed quickly to the safety of French ports.

His most famous battle took place in the North Sea in September 1779. The French had supplied him with an old ship, which he outfitted with forty cannons and named *Bonhomme Richard*, French for *Poor Richard*, the name of the famous almanac written by Benjamin Franklin. Jones also painted the decks of the ship red, so that his crew would not be frightened later when blood began to flow. Jones and the crew of the *Bonhomme Richard* met a large British convoy bringing supplies to their army in America. It seemed at first that the British would win, but Jones refused to surrender, shouting, "I have not yet begun to fight." That gave heart to his men, who fought on and finally defeated the convoy.

After the war ended, Jones was given a gold medal for his bravery. He died while visiting in Europe in 1792, but his body was later brought back to America and buried in the chapel at the U.S. Naval Academy.

CHRONOLOGY

1765	Stamp Act passed, which forced colonists to pay more taxes.
1773, December 16	Boston residents rebel against tax on tea by throwing cargoes of tea into Boston Harbor.
1774	First Continental Congress elected.
1775, April 18–19	Gage leads British troops to Lexington and Concord, where the first shots are fired.
1776, January	Thomas Paine's Common Sense published.
1776, July 4	Continental Congress approves the Declaration of Independence.
1776, September	Nathan Hale captured and hanged by the British.
1778, February	Baron von Steuben begins training Washington's army.
1778, June 28	The Battle of Monmouth fought.
1779, September	John Paul Jones defeats a large British convoy en route to America.
1780	Benedict Arnold commits treason. He agrees to surrender West Point to the British in exchange for money.
1781, October 19	British surrender to Washington at Yorktown, Virginia, ending the war.
1789	George Washington takes office as the nation's first president.

The signing of the Declaration of Independence inspired the colonists in their fight for freedom from British rule.

FOR FURTHER INFORMATION

BOOKS

Susan Provost Belier, *The Revolutionary War*. New York: Benchmark, 2002.

Joy Hakim, *A History of Us: From Colonies to Country—1710–1791*. New York: Oxford University Press, 1999.

Doreen Rappaport and Joan Verniero, *Victory or Death! Stories of the American Revolution*. New York: HarperCollins, 2003.

Gail B. Stewart, *The Importance of Benjamin Franklin*. San Diego, CA: Lucent, 1992.

WEBSITES

Liberty! The American Revolution
www.pbs.org/ktca/liberty
A very exciting site with maps, stories of everyday life in prewar America, and a game users can play online.

The Revolutionary War
www.members.aol.com
Very helpful for research on people, battles, and causes of the war. The Web page links the user to more than seventy-five other sites.

Gail B. Stewart received her undergraduate degree from Gustavus Adolphus College in St. Peter, Minnesota. She did her graduate work in English, linguistics, and curriculum study at the College of St. Thomas and the University of Minnesota. She taught English and reading for more than ten years. She has written more than ninety books for young people, including a series for Lucent Books called The Other America. She has written many books on historical topics such as World War I and the Warsaw ghetto. Stewart and her husband live in Minneapolis with their three sons, Ted, Elliot, and Flynn; two dogs; and a cat. When she is not writing she enjoys reading, walking, and watching her sons play soccer.

INDEX